YOUR KNOWLEDGE HAS VALUE

Bibliographic information published by the German National Library:

The German National Library lists this publication in the National Bibliography; detailed bibliographic data are available on the Internet at http://dnb.dnb.de .

Imprint:

Copyright © 2013 GRIN Verlag, Open Publishing GmbH
Print and binding: Books on Demand GmbH, Norderstedt Germany
ISBN: 978-3-668-09643-1

This book at GRIN:

http://www.grin.com/en/e-book/230335/overview-and-analysis-of-operations-management-lean-operations-quality

James Carter

Overview and Analysis of Operations Management. Lean Operations, Quality Management and Inventory Management

GRIN Publishing

GRIN - Your knowledge has value

Since its foundation in 1998, GRIN has specialized in publishing academic texts by students, college teachers and other academics as e-book and printed book. The website www.grin.com is an ideal platform for presenting term papers, final papers, scientific essays, dissertations and specialist books.

Visit us on the internet:

http://www.grin.com/

http://www.facebook.com/grincom

http://www.twitter.com/grin_com

Table of Contents

Abstract

This essay will analyse the key factors which determine 'success' and 'failure' of quality management (QM), lean operations and inventory management. These three areas of operations management are significant and can dramatically improve a firm's efficiency, responsiveness and reduce costs. This essay will illustrate how theoretical frameworks can help explain the actions of organisations past and present, and the success of these actions will be evaluated.

Managers often fail to understand for operations to be successful, a company wide approach or cultural shift must occur. There is much literature on the application of these operations in a small number of sectors, namely, manufacturing. This essay will analyse the appropriateness of these operations across many sectors and will draw upon case studies as well as my own experience.

Quality Management

Overview

QM is a company wide approach of continuous improvement to enhance the ability to produce high quality products at lower cost (Spector, 1994). It refers to not only the quality of the finished product, as perceived by the consumer, but of the entire corporation (Ishikawa, 1985). The aim of QM is to maximise the "long-term success through customer satisfaction, as well as benefit all members of the organization and society" (ISO 8402, 1992).

TQM became popular in America during the 1980's due to the competitive onslaught of Japanese firms in the electronics and auto industries (Hayes, 1980). This threat and the belief QM can enhance the firm's competitiveness led to a "flurry of activity" (Business Week, 1992) by many organisations in manufacturing, service, profit, and nonprofit industries to adopt QM techniques. In fact 93% of America's largest firms adopted TQM in some form in this period (Little, 2001).

Analysis

Garvin (1984) proposed five approaches to define quality. Firstly, the transcendent approach which is synonymous with innate excellence. This definition of quality cannot be defined, and one can only recognise quality through experience. The second definition is a product based approach where quality is a precise and measurable variable, such as quality ice cream having greater butterfat content. The third definition is a 'user based approach' which users view of quality is subjective; "beauty is in the eye of the beholder. The fourth definition is manufacturing based, viewing quality as conformance to requirements (Crosby, 1979). Any deviation from this suggests defects are created, which should be avoided. The last definition is the value based approach which defines quality in terms of cost and priceindicating quality can be viewed as a measure of worth.

Garvin (1984) identifies eight dimensions of quality: performance, features, reliability, conformance, durability, serviceability, aesthetics, and perceived quality. These dimensions are not necessarily equally weighted for every product. For example, computer chips are deemed 'quality' if they are durable, reliable and conform to specified performance. However, a hand bag's quality may be deemed by its aesthetic appearance alone. For a company to determine their product's quality, they must define quality in their industry, and understand how to measure quality. The company can then set in place controls to ensure consistent quality and minimal defects. A popular method is Total Quality Management (TQM) whicha strategy to enhance competitive performance and better meet the needs of customer while improving the quality of products and operations. TQM is an integrated management philosophy and outlines practices which emphasise continuous improvement, long term thinking, team work, process redesign, and closer suppliers relations (Ross, 1993).

Deming (1982) set out 14 points which he believed would increase the competitiveness of US manufacturing. Deming emphasised the role of management in the successful implementation of TQM as managers can inspire a company-wide cultural shift towards quality. DiMaggio & Powell (1983) support this view and suggest that management must be committed to QM for it to be successful. If TQM is adopted merely to imitate others, the understanding of TQM and how it can improve performance will be low. If understanding is low, commitment will be low, which leads to abandonment. Indeed, The Wallace Company, an oil company in Texas, filed for bankruptcy after winning the Baldrige Award for QM (Hill, 1993).

Juran (1993) argues QM is not simply identifying and reducing variation; it is a company-wide focus to best serve the customer's needs. Grant et al. (1994) goes on to suggest that TQM visions the convergence of the long term interests of customers, employees and shareholders. By increasing quality, organisations can achieve both economic and social goals; reduce costs while benefiting customers through improved performance at a lower price. The authors explain TQM recognises the human need to create; quality has intrinsic value and quality products embody human's quest for perfection. They argue that TQM demonstrates a return to craftsmanship which suffered in the last few decades.

Ford Motor Company utilised strategies including TQM and more recently Six Sigma to increase quality and competitiveness. Ford developed extensive supplier evaluation systems, ensuring consistently quality. As a result, warranty claims declined 60% (Dan Dobbs, Ford Motor Company). Six Sigma, developed by Motorola in 1985, aims to reduce defects in manufactured products. Hong (2003) suggests this strategy works best in repetitive processes, such as high volume car manufacturing which is low variation and low visibility to customers. Deming (1986) put forward the DUMAIC (acronym) methodology of six sigma's implementation. This stands for: define the problem, measure relevant data, analyse data relationships, improve current processes, and lastly: control future processes to ensure variations are corrected before they result in defects. One method of error avoidance is "poka yoke", where processes are designed so that human error is minimised or highly unlikely to occur resulting in fewer defects and increased quality. Examples include visual cues given to factory workers when a computer part has been successfully assembled at that stage of production. These are highly effective measures which reduce waste, however some implementations may increase lead time in some cases.

Quality management and quality control process such as six sigma clearly work well in the manufacturing industry, however some academics question if it is as applicable in other sectors (Naj, 1993). However it is generally agreed that the framework of quality management frameworks can be applied to any industry where customers are involved (Juran, 1993).

Conclusion

The majority of literature suggests (QM) reduces costs, increases market share, customer satisfaction and productivity. Strategies to achieve these include TQM which aims to eliminate waste in production processes. This strategy is particularly effective in low variation processes and has allowed firms including Ford and Toyota to increase the reliability of its cars, a key quality aspect as perceived by its customers. The reduction of variation in the production process is key to delivering quality products to the next downstream customer. Strategies such as SIx Sigma have been utilised successfully to reduce defects and waste. In particular, poka-yoke prevents variations occurring by error proofing processes. The key to their implementation is understanding and measuring relevant data in the operation, as argued by Deming (1986).

Much focus has been made on QM in manufacturing industries, however Naj 1(993) argues that the fundamental frameworks of QM can be applied to any customer oriented sector, including services and retailers. However, successful implementation of QM relies significantly on management's commitment and understanding that QM should implemented as a long term strategy to raise product quality, increase customer satisfaction and increase shareholder value.

Inventory Management

Introduction

Inventory is defined as a stock of items kept on hand to meet customer demand (Russell, 1995). The importance of inventory to a firm arises from financial and operational perspectives. Firstly, inventory represents a major financial outlay for a firm. For manufactures, inventory represents 25 to 50% of total assets, and up to 80% in retailers (Johson et al, 1974). In the operational sense, inventories increase operating flexibility.

Inventory management aims to achieve a balance between low inventory and maximising return on investment (ROI). Inventory ties up working capital and incurs added costs which reduce profit each day excess stock is held. Costs include storage fees, opportunity costs, stockout costs, and administration costs. Good inventory management is therefore crucial to improving customer service and increasing profit margins.

Analysis

Pandey (1990) suggests inventory is manufactured stock for sale and the components that makes up a product. Organisations hold inventory as work in progress (WIP), raw materials, and finished goods. Inventories help protect against risk of unpredictable demand and delivery time, and allows the firm to take advantage of discounts associated with forward buying. However there are two main costs associated with inventories. Firstly, 'carrying costs'; incurred when maintaining any level of inventory and include insurance, tax, storage costs and obsolescence. Carrying costs are significant; costing up to 40% of the value of the inventory itself (Gattorna, 1998). Lucy (1996) suggests these costs will, in the long term, reduce the competitiveness of the firm as prices increase. The second cost is 'stock-out' costs; incurred when there is no inventory which creates production stoppages, opportunity costs, loss of sales and customer dissatisfaction (Pandey, 1999). Therefore firm seek to maximise flexibility by holding inventory, while minimising the costs associated with it.

Umble (2002) suggested the determining factors for successful inventory management. Firstly, top level managers should be committed, as QM requires strong leadership and participation. In order for managers to be committed to inventory management controls, there must be a clear definition of goals and a compelling vision. Secondly, Umble highlights the importance of education and training. She suggests that if employees do not understand the inventory system, they will likely create their own system creating inefficiencies. Thirdly, Umble builds upon prior research by Laughlin (1999) to argue that data accuracy is a critical factor in successful implementation of any inventory management system. Data accuracy is especially critical in the beginning phases of implementing new process, such as Just-In-Time, as employees will have greater trust in the new systems. With more recent development in IT, including RFID, barcodes, handheld computers, data accuracy is increasing accurate and more accessible to a wider range of businesses.

As mentioned, a conflict arises between having enough inventory to maximise flexibility, and minimising inventory to reduce costs. In response, some companies have attempted to optimise the order quantities and order points. Traditionally the solution was to balance the cost of ordering too much and too little. For example, the economic order quantity (EOQ) is determined by balancing ordering costs against carrying costs thereby minimising stocking costs (Harris, 1913). EOQ is primarily used for purchase-to-stock manufacturers and retailers where demand is constant throughout the year and there are fixed costs of ordering. Critics of EOQ suggest it is overly simplistic and cannot be used as prescriptive devices, merely descriptive. Moreover, the real costs of stock in a firm is not assumed (Lonergman, 2001).

The ABC model aims to identify products which will have a significant impact on overall inventory costs. Products are ranked by usage value; items with the highest usage value warrant the closest control, whereas low value items require less control. Typically 80% of an operation's sales are attributed to 20% of all stocked item types (Pareto principle).This model is useful as it allows a firm to reduce costs by adding greater flexibility in the management process.

Just In Time (JIT) aims to reduce waste by minimising inventory. Developed by the Japanese, JIT aims to eliminate all work-in-progress (WIP), and produce only goods that are immediately needed by the customer; thereby removing the cost burden of storing idle parts. However, there may be significant upfront costs to redesign the processes in place. Drury (1990) suggests JIT favour product layouts rather than batch production, and reiterates that JIT is more than an inventory management system; it's a management philosophy to reduce waste in production.

My personal experience of working at Apple has highlighted the benefits of a JIT system when tightly integrated with IT systems, and ABC model. Apple uses IT systems to predict each store's daily demand for products based on seasonality, product launches, and year on year demand figures. Apple classifies products in a similar way to the ABC model, allowing high value products are re-stocked more frequently than low value products. As a product is purchased in store, and if the item is high value, the same item will be delivered from the regional distribution centre the next day. This allows Apple to reduce lead time and maintain a certain buffer stock level in order to satisfy customer demand at all times. Apple currently holds roughly 5 days of inventory, compared to Dell's 10 days and Hewlett Packard's 26. As a result, Apple has minimised inventory while rarely stocking-out. It could be argued the JIT system can increase costs due to more frequent deliveries which can cause complications in Apple's global supply chain.

Conclusion

The literature highlights how effective inventory management systems can reduce inventory costs, increase customer satisfaction (Gattorna, 1998) and lead to greater performance (Baldenius and Reichelstein 2005). It is however difficult to balance the need to have enough buffer stock to maximise flexibility and reduce production risks, with the need minimise stock levels and the costs associated.

Nienhaus et al (2009, p51) identified the greater the lead time between the company and customer, the larger the variation in demand. For example OEMs experience lower demand variability compared to 3rd tier suppliers. This is known as the 'bull whip' effect, and indicates that the success of inventory management systems, such as JIT or EOQ depends largely upon the company and their supplier relationships, ability to predict demand levels, and their proximity with the end customer.

Lean operations

Introduction

The growing pressure to become efficient and competitive has led organisations to implement waste reduction strategies in production processes (Kinnie et al., 1996). 'Lean' describes the ability to do more with less i.e improved resource utilisation. Toyota was key in developing this practice. In the 1940s, Toyota's diverged from American mass production techniques as they faced limited financial resources, fragmented and scarce human and natural resources, and the limited availability of land. Toyota's concept, 'Toyota Production System' (TPS), solved this problem and significantly reduced manufacturing costs and increased profit margin by reducing waste at every stage of production. By the late 1980s, the benchmark study by Womack found Toyota was superior to the competition on almost every exercise they conducted as a result of TPS (Womack and Jones, 1996).

The Manufacturing Research Centre (2005) found lean operations to be an essential part of the manufacturing process. Moreover, with current world uncertainties, such as supply chain disruptions, lean operations is increasingly important to increase responsiveness.

Analysis

Lean is thought of as a philosophy rather than a tool, utilised by manufacturers, retailers, and any service where customers are involved and the common goal is to eliminate waste and non-value added tasks Womack et al. (1990). The principles of lean operations include the efficient use of resources, teamwork, communication and continuous improvement (Kaizen). According to Marchwinski and Shook (2004), lean operations is a way of organising operations with fewer resources, less capital, and less time to produce goods with fewer defects compared with traditional mass production; characterised by high production volumes, long non-value added queue times, and large batch sizes.

Womack suggests 'lean' aims to reduce lead times by eliminating waste ("muda" in Japanese), and is synonymous with Toyota's Production System (TPS) and Just in Time (JIT). JIT is a 'pull' system and allows organisations to produce only what is required at that moment in time. This allows stock levels of WIP, raw materials finished goods can be kept to a minimum. JIT requires sophisticated scheduling systems to plan production and ordering points, ideally suited for manufactures and some retailers. Made-to-order (MTO) operations are applied wherever possible. In the PC business, for example, MTO production is often the de facto business model. Dell's 'direct sales model' produces PCs as the customer places the order. This model allows Dell to customise each PC to the customer's specification.

Mehara and Inman (1992) studied the critical factors of success and failures of JIT systems. Contrary to popular belief, it was found that management commitment to JIT implementation was not a critical factor to the success of JIT. Their study may be inconclusive though as the perception of commitment was tested rather than empirical data. Bandyopadhyay (2004) further studied managerial commitment, and suggested it is infact the most significant factor of JITs success, although noted JIT must be a company wide initiative rather than just apply to parts of a business; agreeing with Mehara and Inman's findings (1992).

Achanga et al. (2005) found an organisation's financial capacity is crucial in determining the success of implementing lean operations. In their study of small and medium enterprises (SMEs), they found implementing lean operations requires significant financial resources to hire consultants, retrain staff, and implement new processes. These findings suggest that adopting lean strategies may be daunting for SMEs, particularly as they lack the necessary financial resources and cannot easily afford breaks in production to retrain staff. For this reason, the study suggests lean may be better suited for larger firms with greater financial capacity.

Studies have been made on the success of lean in non manufacturing sectors. Arnheiter et al., (2005) suggested that the lean's fundamental philosophy of reducing waste and adding customer value can be easily applied to other sectors including banking, medicine and virtually any service where customers are involved. In the 1980s, Taco Bell identified issues in their operations, such as employees were frequently being decoupled and were required to fulfil multiple roles, such as serving customers and making food. This was a highly inefficient process (Schlesinger and Heskett, 1991). By the 1990s, Taco Bell better understood its customer's needs: fast service, hot food, clean environment and accurate orders. They allowed customer pull demand in a production to service process, which resulted in the kitchen space being reduced to 30% of total area, thereby maximising the restaurant's capacity. Taco Bell use JIT deliveries of pre-processed materials; reducing WIP inventory, saving space and reducing costs. Taco Bell were successful in implementing lean operations in order to become for customer focussed, although Schlesinger highlights that the success was due to the adoption of advanced lean production technologies including value-chain analysis, JIT, and investments in human capital.

Investing in human capital is a significant contributor to the success of lean operations (Abdi et al., 2006). As inefficiencies in human capital are regarded as waste, emphasis should be placed on hiring the right people for a particular role. Moreover, the authors argue ongoing investments in retraining workers is key to reduce waste in the operation, an approach consistent with Kaizen or 'constant improvement'. Emiliani (2001) argues that a fundamental reason for lean failing is the inability to retrain workers and make constant investments in their skills. He identifies that many companies layoff workers in an effort to cut waste, however he suggests that workers should be retrained and assigned to value adding operations. This is a strong argument, and retraining costs should be viewed as long term investments to increase efficiency.

Conclusion

Lean operations has wide benefits however faces many challenges in practice. The benefits of lean operations include reduced demand variability, increased responsiveness, reduced lead time, minimal inventory and reduced costs.

The key success factors include commitment by management, although the strength of this factor was questioned Mehara and Inman (1992). It would be interesting to see further research made in this area. Other factors leading to successful implementation of 'lean' include strong financial capacity and investment.

Overall, the literature indicates that lean operations is a highly valuable and can be incorporated in a wide variety of business types, not only manufacturing as commonly believed. Lean operations and strategies such as JIT should be used as part as a wider consideration by the whole company to reduce waste at all stages of production.

BIBLIOGRAPHY

(2005) Leaning on uncertainty. *The Manufacturer.* 10 June ed.

(1996) "Lean and its limits". *Economist,* Vol 340, No 7983, 65.

(1992). The quality imperative: What it takes to win for the global economy. Business Week [Special issue]. October 25: 1-216.

Abdi, F; Shavarini, Sohrab K; Hoseini, Seyed, M. (2006) Glean Lean: How to Use Lean Approach in Service Industries? Journal of Services Research, Volume 6,

Achanga, P., Shehab, E., Roy, R., & Nelder, G. (2006). Critical success factors for lean implementation within SMEs. Journal of Manufacturing Technology Management, 17(4), 460-471.

Arnheiter, E.D, Maleyeff, J., (2005) "The integration of lean management and Six Sigma", The TQM Magazine, Vol. 17 Iss: 1, pp.5 - 18

Baldenius, T. and Reichelstein S. (2005): Incentives for Efficient Inventory Management: The Role of Historical Cost, *Management Science.*, 51(7).

Beer, M. (2003) Why total quality management programs do not persist: The role of management quality and implications for leading a TQM transformation. *Decision Science.* Volume 34, 4.

Bremner, B. & Dawson, C. (2003) "Can anything stop Toyota?" *Business Week,* Vol November 17th, No 3858, 114-122.

Bandyopadhyay, J. (2004) Implementing Just In Time Production and Procurement Strategies. International Journal of Management Vol. 12 No.1

Crosby, P. B. (1974) *Quality Is Free* (New York: McGraw-Hill, 1979); Gilmore.

Cusumano, M. A. & Nobeoka, K. (1998) Thinking Beyond Lean: How Multi- Project Management is Transforming Product Development at Toyota and Other Companies, New York, The Free Press.

Dan Dobbs (2011), 6-Sigma Master Black Belt at Ford Motor Company.

Deming, W. E. (1986) *Out of the crisis.* Cambridge, MA: Massachusetts Institute of Technology, Center for Advanced Engineering Study.

DiMaggio, P. J., & Powell, W. W. (1983). The iron cage revisited: Institutional isomorphism and collective rationality in organisational field. *American Sociological Review,* 48, 147-160.

Drury, C. (1990). Counting the Cost of AMT Investment. Journal of Accountancy, April, pp.134-138.

Emiliani, M.L. (2001), "Redefining the focus of investment analysts", The TQM Magazine, Vol. 13 No. 1, pp. 34-50.

Evans, J. R., Anderson, D. R., Sweeney, D. J., and Williams, T. A. (1990). Applied Production and Operations Management. West Publishing Company.

Gattorna, J. (1998) Strategic supply chain alignment. Gower publishing ltd, Hampshire, England.

Grant, R., Shani, R. and Krishnan, R. (1994), TQM's challenge to management theory and practice', *Sloan Management Review*, Vol. 35 No. 2, pp. 25-35.

Johson R. A., Newell, W. T. & Vergin, R. C. (1974). Production and Operations Management. Houghton Mifflin Company.

Juran, J. (1993). 'Made in U.S.A.: A renaissance in quality'. Harvard Business Review, pp. 42-50.

Kinnie, N., Hutchninson, S., Purcell, J., Rees, C., Scarbrough, H. and Terr, M. (1996), The People Management Implications of Leaner Working, Institute of Personnel Management, London.

Harris F W (1913), "How Many Parts to Make at Once in Factory", *The Magazine of Management*, Vol. 10, No. 2, pp. 136-152.

Hayes, R. & W. Abernathy (1980). Managing our way to economic decline. *Harvard Business Review*, pp. 67-77.

Ishikawa, K. (1985), What is Total Quality Control, Prentice-Hall, New York, NY.

Hill, R. (1993). *When the going gets tough:* A Baldridge Award winner on the line', *The Executive,* 7(3), pp75-79.

Hong, G.Y., T.N. Goh, (2003) Six Sigma in software quality, *The TQM Magazine*, Vol. 15 Iss: 6, pp.364 - 373

Goldratt, E. M. (1997) *Critical Chain*, Gower Publishing Limited.

Hendricks, K. B., & Singhal, V. (2001) The long run stock price performance of firms with effective TQM programs. *Management Science*, 47, 359-368.

Hopp, W.J. and Spearman, M.L. (2001), Factory Physics, 2nd ed., Irwin/McGraw-Hill, New York, NY, p. 25.

Inman, R.R. (1999), Are you implementing a pull system by putting the cart before the horse?, Production and Inventory Management Journal, Vol. 40 No. 2, pp. 67-71.

Laughlin, S. (1999) An ERP game plan, Journal of Business Strategy. January-February, 32-37.

Lonergan E. (2001) "Introduction supply and materials management'', Gps London.

Lucy, T. & Drury, C. (1995) *Costing* 4th edition. D.P Publications

Marchwinski, Chet and Shook, John; (2004); Lean Lexicon – A graphical glossary for Lean Thinkers; Second Edition, Version 2.0; Brookline, MA, USA

Mehra, S., & Inman, R. A. (1992). Determining the critical elements of just-in-time implementation. *Decision Sciences*, *23*(1), 160-174.

Naj, A. (1993) *Some manufactures drop efforts to adopt Japanese manufacturing techniques.* Wall Street Journal, p.A1.

Nienhaus, J., Ziegenbein, A., Schoensleben, P., 2006. How human behaviour amplifies the bullwhip effect. A study based on the beer distribution game online. Production Planning & Control 17, 547–557.

Pandey, I.M. (1999) "Financial management'' 7 edition, Vikas publishing house, PVT ltd

Powell, C. (1995) Total quality management as competitive advantage: A review and empirical study. *Strategic Management Journal.* Volume 16, 1. 15-37.

Rangaraj N, Raghuram G and Srinivasan M M (2009) *Supply Chain Management for Competitive Advantage: Concepts and Cases*, 1st Edition, Tata Mcgraw-Hill Publishing Company Limited, New Delhi.

Ross, J. (1993) *Total Quality Management: Text Cases and Readings.* St. Lucie Press, Delray Beach, FL

Russell, R. S. & Taylor, B. W. (1995). Production and Operations Management. Prentice-Hall, Inc.

Schein, E. H. (1992). *Organisational culture and leadership: San Francisco :* Jossey-Bass.

Schlesinger, L.A. and Hallowell, R.H. (1994) 'Taco Bell Corporation: a case of service leadership', Proceedings of QUIS-3, Quality in Services Conference, International Service Quality Association, pp. 247-257.

Shirouzo, N. A. M., S. (2004) "As Toyota Closes In on GM, Quality Concerns Also Grow". *Wall Street Journal - Eastern Edition,* Vol 244, No 24.

Spector, B., & Beer, M. (1994). Beyond TQM programs. *Journal of Organisational Change Management,* 7(2), 63-70.

Umble, E. J., Haft, R. R., & Umble, M. M. (2003). Enterprise resource planning: Implementation procedures and critical success factors. European Journal of Operational Research, 146(2), 241-257.

Walton, M. (1986). *The Deming Management Method,* Pedigree, New York.

Womack, J. P. & Jones, D. T. (1996) "Lean Thinking", New York, New York, Simon & Schuster Ltd.